– ABOUT THE AUTHORS –

WILLIAM GLASSER, M.D., is a board certified psychiatrist who developed reality therapy, an effective counseling technique. Reality therapy eventually evolved into choice theory, which is described in this book. Both are now recognized and taught around the world.

CARLEEN GLASSER, M.A., works with her husband teaching relationship workshops and choice theory seminars using the ideas Dr. Glasser has developed. She has been an instructor for the William Glasser Institute for twenty years.

Both have extensive experience in counseling but are spending much of their time now working together lecturing, writing, and teaching. This book is the most recent product of that effort.

Eight Lessons for a Happier Marriage

BOOKS BY WILLIAM GLASSER, M.D., AND CARLEEN GLASSER, M.A.

OTHER BOOKS BY WILLIAM GLASSER, M.D.

Warning: Psychiatry Can Be Hazardous to Your Health
For Parents and Teenagers
Counseling with Choice Theory
Reality Therapy in Action
The Quality School Teacher
Choice Theory in the Classroom
Choice Theory
Staying Together (Revised as: *Getting Together and Staying Together*)
The Control Theory Manager
The Quality School
Control Theory in the Classroom
Control Theory
Schools Without Failure
Reality Therapy
Positive Addiction
The Identity Society
Mental Health or Mental Illness?
Stations of the Mind

EIGHT LESSONS

LESSONS

– FOR A –

HAPPIER MARRIAGE

William Glasser, M.D.,
and Carleen Glasser, M.A.

HARPER

NEW YORK · LONDON · TORONTO · SYDNEY

HARPER

On the Edge cartoons are used with permission of the copyright holders Joe Martin and Neatly Chiseled Features.

The individuals featured throughout this book are composites of patients the author has counseled or known in the course of his professional career. Any resemblance to actual persons, living or dead, is purely coincidence.

HarperCollins books may be purchased for educational, business, or sales promotional use. For information please write: Special Markets Department, HarperCollins Publishers, 10 East 53rd Street, New York, NY 10022.

FIRST EDITION

Designed by Jaime Putorti

Library of Congress Cataloging-in-Publication Data
is available upon request.
ISBN: 978-0-06-133692-8
ISBN-10: 0-06-133692-0

07 08 09 10 11   ❖/RRD   10 9 8 7 6 5 4 3 2 1

To our married children
Alice and Jesse
Martin and Pamela
Jana and Michael
Terry and Barbara G.

May you each live a long and happy life together!

— ACKNOWLEDGMENTS —

We want to thank all the married couples we have known throughout our lives. Some were happy, others were not, but we learned a great deal from all of them. They inspired us to write this book.

We acknowledge and thank Joe Martin and Jon Carlson for allowing us to use their great cartoons and wise comments. We appreciate Brandi Roth and Bruce Clemens for their endless patience and generosity of their time and their friendship. Finally, for her tremendous insight and her continuing dedication and support, we thank and appreciate Linda Harshman. We could not have done this without her help.

– CONTENTS –

Contents

LESSON SIX

LESSON SEVEN

LESSON EIGHT

– ILLUSTRATIONS –

– PREFACE –

William and Carleen Glasser have combined their knowledge of functioning marriages and failed marriages, all under the umbrella of William Glasser's Choice Theory, to present *Eight Lessons for a Happier Marriage*. *Eight Lessons* begins with the fundamental truth that the only person you can change is yourself. You cannot make your spouse change. The more you try, the more unhappiness you create. *Eight Lessons* builds on that foundation with the elements of successful marriages, the elements of failed marriages, and the insight to recognize the differences. Correcting an off-course marriage may only require a few adjustments. The secret is recognizing the adjustments that can be made and not attempting to force adjustments that cannot be forced.

This book is clear, direct, and accessible. A great concept does not require a lot of words.

I have been a divorce lawyer for thirty years. I have represented many people with great wealth whose marital problems were not financial and for whom no amount of money could fix those problems. In *Eight Lessons*, I recognize the patterns of marital failure that I have seen over and over. I suspect that many of those failed marriages could have been saved if those couples had read and applied the *Eight Lessons* long before their marriages had withered.

Bruce A. Clemens, Esq.
Beverly Hills, California
2007

– FOREWORD –

"I THINK I CAN DO BETTER, SHOULD I SETTLE FOR SECOND BEST?"
The real question is, can YOU be a different partner? Most of the time we believe that we're wonderful and all we need to do is find a better partner. The truth is we need to BE a better partner.

All people begin marriage with high hopes for a lifetime of "happy togetherness." Soon the couple realizes that their expectations are beyond possibility (at least with this partner!). What began as joy soon turns to disappointment and loneliness. Many couples choose to end their marriages and soon begin the same cycle again.

Marriage is for better **and** worse. Too many couples quit, however, without realizing that things will soon return from worse to better. Recent research shows that three out of four divorcing couples who decide to stay married report satisfaction in their relationship five years later. Many of these couples even had serious external problems like infidelity, physical abuse, poverty, and alcoholism. They were able to improve when they honored their original commitment to stay together "until death do us part." The sad part is that those who divorce seldom find that level of "satisfaction."

There is so little focus on making one's partner happy. Instead, we look to our partners to make us happy and we may even believe that it is their responsibility to do so. We try to control, coerce, humble, guilt, shame, and do whatever else we can think of to get what *we* want from the marriage. We each become very clear about what our partner needs to do to improve but seem oblivious of the need to change ourselves. This book helps partners to take responsibility for their role in creating marital misery and unhappiness. The authors not only present ideas but even make the necessary tools available in each of the eight lessons.

I have had the very good fortune to have known Bill and Carleen Glasser for several years. We have had opportunities to teach, travel, and create professional media projects together. The Glassers realize that decisions need to be made on the basis of what is best for *us*. They realize the importance of using words like *we, us,* and *ours* to frequently solidify marriage as a true partnership.

This small book is powerful because it shows the practical wisdom that comes only with age and experience. As I read through the book, I was reminded of the story about Occam's razor: Complex problems really do not always need complex solutions. The ideas in this book are clearly stated, and the examples are simply told. Consider rereading the book each month as a means to help stay on the relationship course you have chosen. I would also recommend that you do the Skit if you have children; it will significantly reduce the stresses that result from our better **and** worse relationships.

The Glassers are strong believers that mental health is the result of getting along with all the important people in your life. The ideas presented in this book are tailored for marriage but will apply to all other relationships. As the comedian Jonathan Winters stated, "If your ship doesn't come in . . . then swim out to it." Follow the Glassers' example and take responsibility for choosing a healthy and happy path with all of your relationships.

Jon Carlson, PsyD, EdD, ABPP
Distinguished Professor
Governors State University
Author of Time for a Better Marriage

Eight Lessons for a Happier Marriage

– INTRODUCTION –

Essentially, we all get married. We've been doing it for eons all over the world, and there's no indication we are going to stop. Many of us divorce and marry again— sometimes several times. Unmarried people often yearn for marriage, and many who are married yearn for freedom. But after a period of freedom most try marriage again, even though marriage is not what they really want.

What they want the first time and every time, and almost always experience, is a delightful pre- and postmarriage interval called infatuation, which they believe is love. While they are infatuated, they totally accept each other, both socially and sexually, and fervently hope this feeling will last forever, seemingly unaware of the harsh reality that infatuation is not love.

Infatuation begins to fade as the couple learns more about each other. As disheartening as this is at the time, the loss of infatuation seems no deterrent to this relentless process. When this happens, most couples believe that they have actually stopped loving each other and start thinking about going their own way instead of making the effort to learn how to move from infatuation to lasting love.

There are some successful first marriages but not that many. Living happily ever after for a lifetime is more fantasy than fact because couples give up too soon after infatuation dies. But as a good friend of mine, who was married several times before a fourth marriage succeeded, said, "Consider the alternative." In his case he finally got lucky, but in our opinion, there has never been a need-satisfying alternative to a happy marriage. Being lonely and single was for him and is for a vast majority of the rest of us just plain miserable. There are, of course, some exceptions to this preference. A few people are satisfied with staying single and find their own happiness. But it is an undeniable fact that unhappy marriage, with all its fallout, is a huge problem all over the world with seemingly few solutions in sight. A good way to conceive of this is to visualize ourselves as human lemmings walking off a long gently sloping cliff. A few stop walking but are still very much aware of the uncomfortable slope they are standing on. It's an effort to stay there, and the effort drains our strength. Only a few of us are able to learn how to turn our brief infatuation into the long-term sexual friendship we call love, figure out how to stay happily married, and never start down that fatal slope.

But while we still have some strength, quite a few of us turn around and walk back up the slope hoping to meet a new exciting lemming and reexperience the infatuation we had before. Many of us find someone, and the infatuation we once had returns with a new but in many ways similar partner. But if we can't figure out how to turn this new infatuation into love, which only a few of us can, the new lemming we find soon becomes a too-familiar copy of the former spouse and we are back on the slope again. This unhappy ritual may be repeated several times, but the general trend is downhill.

When one or both partners go their own way, many turn to affairs. Infidelity, a solution to the familiarity problem for centuries in all cultures, has many advocates. The initial marriage stays intact, but one or both partners have another or other sexual outlets. Traditionally, the man strays and the woman stays home with the children. But there are many variations. The only variation that may work for some couples is when they both believe that their marriage should take precedence over what the partners do with others. But this is a rare variation. In most instances, the wife and family suffer while the husband roams. It is very rare that any deviation from a loving long-term marriage can be free of problems.

In this book we will explain in detail what we have learned both from personal experience and from years of observing the marriages of many couples who are unhappily married but who for a variety of good reasons do not want to divorce. Rather than counsel them, which traditionally is an attempt to fix their marriage, we have set out to teach both partners how to work together to create a happy marriage based on a new theory we call choice theory.

If you read each lesson together willingly, talk it over, and try to put the information in the lesson to work in your marriage, you should be able to enhance your marital happiness. The eight lessons become a marriage enrichment experience. As you go through the book, each of you will learn how to behave differently with each other than you are behaving now, and this way will be different from how almost all married couples have behaved with each other for thousands of years. From our experience, while the lessons will be new to you, they are neither difficult to understand nor complicated to put into practice.

Still, what could make them seem difficult for you is that you will be taught to treat each other in ways that may not seem right to you or even fair. But keep in mind that what you have been doing that may seem so right to both of you now has landed you on that slippery slope with the other lemmings. As you put what we are teaching you into practice, you will begin to realize that you are getting along better with your mate than you have in a long time. Unlike dieting and exercising which are tedious at best, these lessons are very pleasant. There is no hurry. Take your time. Think about the difference between our teaching and what you have been doing since your early infatuation faded away.

Finally, there is a lot to learn in the eight lessons, so don't be discouraged. You don't have to learn immediately all there is in the eight lessons in order to get a lot of help. If all both of you can learn is the material in the first lesson, you will have learned a lot more about marriage than most couples on the slippery slope ever learn.

We invite you to start by reading this short book together, and you will begin to get the idea. Then go back to lesson one and spend a lot of time working on getting external control out of your marriage. There is no mystery here. External control is tangible. Every little bit you can remove from your marriage will have a payoff in happiness. Keep in mind that you have spent a lot of time practicing how to be miserable. Learning to be happy together will take a little time too.

Throughout the book you will meet a variety of married couples who will each tell you their story. You will hear both the husband's and the wife's side. They will be perfectly candid because neither will know what the other said. Each of their stories presents problems relating to the issues addressed in the lessons that follow. We use these problems as examples throughout the lesson to help you understand how the information presented can be applied in their marriage. Even though in the lesson we may not discuss their specific problems, we do address the root causes and offer strategies that they or anyone with similar problems could use. Remember, in this book you will be educating yourselves and figuring out how to solve your own marital problems by learning how to change the ways you relate to each other.

"HOW CAN I KEEP THE HOUSE CLEAN WITH-OUT WHINING AND COMPLAINING ALL DAY?" "God made dirt, so dirt don't hurt." As Phyllis Diller stated, "Cleaning the house before your kids are done growing is like shoveling the walk before it stops snowing." Lower your expectations and watch your sanity return!!

John and Meredith's Story

Hi, I'm John, and the trouble with our marriage is Meredith. She's a total control freak. She treats me like I'm her kid. We don't have any of our own, so that's probably why. She has to have the house spotlessly clean all the time. Whenever the house gets dirty, she blames me. You know what she's started doing? She puts Handi Wipes, all opened up and everything, right next to my hands at the breakfast table while I'm reading the newspaper. She expects me to wipe the newsprint off my fingers before I leave the table. She says I get black finger- prints all over the house if I don't.

She's always inspecting me for flaws, a wrinkle in my shirt, lint on my jacket, or a hair out of place. I'm telling you she's driving me nuts. I don't think I can take it anymore. You know what she did the other day? She took all of my old clothes out of my closet and gave them to the Good Will without even checking with me first. She threw out some of my favorite stuff. Said it was collecting dirt.

I get home from work about a half hour before she gets home so I sit down to watch a little TV and have a snack. I'm starving, so I forget to put napkins down all over the place. She comes in and catches me, says I'm making a big mess again. I get so mad I just clam up. Then she asks me about my day. I say, what do you want to know for? So you can tell me every- thing I did wrong.

She gets dinner ready. She's a good cook, and at least I know my food is real clean. We eat together in silence, but as soon as I finish a course, she gets right up and takes my plate into the kitchen and washes it thoroughly before she puts it in the dishwasher. She's up and down so much we don't have time to talk.

Our sex life, that's another story. If she's not mad at me for violating her sanitation rules, she's usually up for it, but by then I don't feel like it. By the end of the day I'm so sick of her bossiness I just want to go to sleep.

The thing is she has a lot of good points. She wasn't like this before we got married. If she would just relax a little bit, I think we could make a go of this marriage. I don't know what to say to her to get her to stop trying to control everything I do. I just wish she'd leave me alone.

※

My name is Meredith, and I'm married to John. He's actually a very sweet, adorable guy. His only problem is he's an absolute and utter slob. I've never in my life seen anybody so sloppy. He can't eat anything without dropping it all over himself. He actually misses his mouth when he tries to put food in.

And then there are his infernal fingerprints. His hands seem to pick up dirt everywhere, and he deposits it all over my house in little black marks. The walls, the doors, the cabinets, are all full of black spots. I go bonkers running around cleaning up after him. He doesn't even know he's doing it. Either he doesn't see it or he doesn't care.

That's it. Sometimes I feel like he doesn't love me enough to do what I want. I don't know how his mother could put up with him and his mess. I once asked her and she seemed offended. Don't ask me why. I was just trying to help him. Maybe she thought I felt it was her fault. To tell you the truth, I guess I do think it's her fault. How could any mother allow her son never to learn basic cleanliness and neatness? I certainly haven't been able to get him to learn it. Lord knows I keep trying.

Other than that, we have a good life. We both have good jobs. We have a nice starter house that I fixed up to look really attractive. Our finances are in really good shape, thanks to me. I keep all the books, write the checks, and pay bills online. I've even invested our savings wisely so we have a little nest egg.

John's great with money. He never spends more than we make, and he really is pretty undemanding. He seems happy with the little pocket money I budgeted for us. In that department I'm happy, but I still get a sense that he doesn't appreciate all the things I do to keep the house clean.

On a scale of one to ten, our sex life is about a four. Lately John doesn't seem to be as interested in me as he used to be. I don't know why. I should be the one who's turned off. I've told him time and again that I'd enjoy it more if he'd take a shower first before he came to bed. He says he doesn't feel like it, but then he asks me to give him oral sex. I think that's disgusting. I wouldn't mind doing it if he'd clean himself first. I even offered to come into the shower with him and wash it for him. He got mad at me for that and said I keep treating him like a baby. I don't know why we're having so much trouble.

– LESSON ONE –
External Control Can Kill a Marriage

Now that you have read John and Meredith's stories we would like to teach you the first lesson of this book. While we can't guarantee success, if you both believe—despite a great many marital problems including infidelity or even an incident or two of abusive behavior—there is still some love left in your marriage, what we will teach you will help. But what we teach will take some effort on both your parts. Depending on the life you have been choosing to live, some partners will have a harder time with this material than others. Certainly, Meredith might have trouble with this information. Our advice is to be patient with yourself and with each other.

What you will actually learn is how to treat, not only each

other, but all the important people in your life differently from the way almost all of you were treated as children. What will be difficult for many of you to learn is that, no matter how others treat you, we will teach both of you not to return their treatment in kind.

We see you as people who were happy together at the start of your marriage, like Meredith and John, but are now in a long-term unsatisfying relationship. Like most unhappy couples, you have both complained about your marriage and blamed each other for your unhappiness, but neither of you understands exactly what went wrong and you have no idea what to do about it. You have thought about separation or divorce, but for many reasons—children, money, family, religion, or fear of starting over by yourself— you have stayed together. You also may believe that the misery of staying together is preferable to the unknowns of separation.

After many years of teaching couples better ways to treat each other in their marriage, we have come to the following three conclusions which are the core beliefs of what we teach— regardless of how unhappy the couples are.

First: All the couples who come to seek our help are unhappy. But as miserable as you are, we do not believe there is anything wrong with either of your brains. An unhappy brain is perfectly capable of creating a huge range of psychological symptoms, such as depression, anger, anxiety, or pain, but neither of you needs psychiatric medication. In fact, if one or both of you are on psychiatric medication, its adverse effect on your brain may be part of your problem.

As a board-certified psychiatrist, I have never prescribed psychiatric medication for unhappiness, and I have no intention of starting now by recommending it to you. If you will keep this first core belief in mind—that you are unhappy but you are capable of learning how to be much happier with each other than you are now—we are on our way.

Second: When we are in an unhappy marriage, in almost all instances we blame our partner for our unhappiness. This blaming will actually increase your unhappiness. We will not talk about fault. The problem you have is neither new nor your fault. Like Meredith and John, it is how you choose to relate to each other in your marriage. It is essentially how all unhappy couples relate as they, like lemmings, travel down that slippery slope.

Third: Both partners are using a world psychology that we call external control. It is a world psychology because almost all human beings marry, and when they have difficulty with each other in the marriage, they all employ this psychology. The use of this psychology is by far the main source of marital unhappiness. It is also the main source of all human unhappiness, but in this book we will focus on you and your marriage.

We call this destructive psychology external control because using it, the husband (who is external to his wife) may try to control her, and the wife (who is external to her husband) may try to control him just as Meredith is trying to control John. The symptoms one or both of you suffer from—for example, depression, anxiety, anger, and fear—are caused by your unsuccessful attempt to control the other, your unsuccessful attempt to escape from the control of the other, or as in many instances both attempts going on at the same time.

Although **external control** is by far the main source of all marital unhappiness, we are almost certain that very few people in the world have any idea how damaging this psychology is to their relationship. Let us begin by explaining that a psychology is a very common way we relate to each other. There are many psychologies we employ when we are getting along well with each other, such as the caring and supporting psychology we call love. Or the caring and encouraging psychology that permeates the relationship between a teacher and a pupil immersed in successful learning.

External control is a psychology in which people who practice it always know what is right for other people. Because they know what is right, they feel obligated to try to coerce others to behave the way they want. This coercive psychology is so universally accepted that almost all married people in every culture on Earth use it as soon as the infatuation ends. That is when they start to try to control the other or escape from the other's control. The less successful they are, the more difficult the marriage gets and the more they use this psychology.

Even if the couple stays together, all the love and even friendship is soon drained from the marriage. Although millions of married people firmly believe in external control, it has no upside. It indiscriminately harms every marriage in which it is employed.

Later in this book we will explain why everybody uses external control, but here we want to alert you to what it is so that you can recognize it as you use it in your marriage. As we will also explain later, it is exclusively a human psychology; no other creature uses it.

Archie Bunker was the epitome of external control as he repeatedly derided his son-in-law, who was trying to live without it. The war between people who use external control and those who resist it is the core of what we call drama, both comedy and tragedy. If people got along well, there would be more creative kinds of humor, such as the stories told by Mark Twain, which would elicit gales of laughter.

Think of a time in your life when you asked your wife to do something she didn't want to do. She did it cheerfully the first time you asked. But then you kept asking, and her good cheer turned into an angry argument. Of course, if you threatened her with physical or mental harm, she might give in and do what you wanted. But she wouldn't do it willingly. If this continued, the relationship between you would be further harmed and eventually destroyed.

If your use of external control has transgressed to physical or emotional violence, then you seriously need help. If you are being abused, report it immediately to people who can help you. Your basic need for safety and possibly even survival is being violated in this abusive relationship. Act now. Call the domestic violence hotline at 1–800–978–3600.

External control is a plague on our whole society. Yet it continues to be used in marriage because everyone who uses it believes he or she is right. The comic parody of the golden rule is *He who has the gold makes the rules*. External control has cost the lives of at least a billion people in the twentieth century, and it's off to a good start in the twenty-first.

You may be a firm believer in external control and an expert in its use, but you don't have to choose to use it in your marriage. Therefore, the specific question for Lesson One is **If your mate continually tries to control you, what could you do that would help your marriage?** Talk to each other about what you honestly believe. This is what Meredith and John did, and it is beginning to help.

Please don't read Lesson Two until you have talked about this question. As in many questions in this book, there is no correct answer. But some ideas are much more effective than others. You'll know which ones they are by the way you both feel about your marriage after you answer them.

ON THE EDGE
with Earl, Nadine & Weederman

BY JOE MARTIN & DR. JON CARLSON

SEVENTEEN ARRESTS, SEVENTEEN CONVICTIONS...

MAYBE IT IS ME!

"WHY IS IT ALWAYS MY FAULT?"
MAYBE IT IS YOU!? If it walks like a duck, sounds like a duck and looks like a duck, maybe you're a duck! Contrary to popular opinion, it is possible to be wrong all the time. Most people have learned to "duck" responsibility by blaming someone or something for problems that can only be fixed by them. Try taking the blame one time, and see what happens.

Tom and Janet's Story

Ever since I've known Tom, he's been telling me what to do. It's as if it never occurs to him that I have a mind of my own. He's constantly monitoring me. He watches everything I do to make sure it's done his way. The way he does it is interesting. For example, he asks me to go to the hardware store and pick up something that seems so simple, like a rake for the garden, or to the market to pick up a honeydew melon. If I ask him questions, he'll explain in great detail what he wants, and I will carefully follow his instructions to the letter.

But as soon as he comes home and sees what I bought, he

invariably says I bought the wrong thing. With Tom I can't get anything right. It's not as if he's mean, but he treats me like I'm an incompetent fool, and then he keeps reminding me about my mistakes. No matter what is going on, he's never wrong and I'm never right.

Then there's the money. We have plenty of it, but no matter what I buy, I spent too much. Even if I've shopped very carefully for something I bought for myself with my own money, which really has nothing to do with him, he'll notice I have something new on and ask me where I bought it, or why I needed it, or how much it cost, and then proceed to tell me what's wrong with it.

It's the same with the children. This has been going on since they were little. Now they're grown and have children of their own. They call and keep me posted about what they're up to, and when I tell him what they said, he tells me they shouldn't have done it that way. He wants me to consult him about their decisions in their private lives. It's gotten so bad, I tell the children not to tell me any of their business because when he asks me, I'll have to listen to his version of what I should have told them to do. He's so bossy our youngest daughter can't stand to talk to him anymore. Why can't he just mind his own business?

I have a lot of aches and pains, and he is very solicitous and wants to get involved in my health problems. He always knows what's best for me and makes sure I follow the doctor's orders exactly. If I don't feel good, his answer is always that I try to do too much and I should let him do it because he can do it so much better than me. It's not that he doesn't love me. He loves me too much and wants to do everything for me. He isn't happy unless he's in charge of everything and everybody.

Frankly, I don't know what to do with him anymore. When he was working, he ran a big company. He would spend most of his energy telling his employees what to do. But now that he's retired, he spends all of his time trying to micromanage me and everyone else we know. Our friends think it's funny, but believe me, I don't. I have to live with him every day.

Don't get me wrong, I love him. He's a good man in many ways, but he's driving me crazy. He makes me so mad sometimes I could scream. Once in a while I do scream at him, and you'd think I'd committed a felony. Then he gives me the silent treatment and ignores me for a couple of days until he stops stewing over it. I'm sure I hurt his feelings when I blow up at him, but once he begins to talk to me, it's the same thing all over again.

✳

Janet and I were high school sweethearts. She was the cutest little thing you ever did want to see. She went to junior college for two years, and we got married right after I got my B.A. in business. So, basically, we were just a couple of kids who didn't know anything. I pretty much had to take over and run the show. I started managing the little business my dad left me, and I made it grow to what it is today. We worked hard, raised three kids, and now we're sitting pretty.

It seems like this should be the happiest time of our lives, but lately Janet seems to be slipping. She doesn't seem to be able to get anything right anymore. Her health hasn't been the greatest, she has a lot of aches and pains, but she doesn't seem to want my help. I'm more than willing to take over here, but the more I try, the less she cooperates.

Last week she screamed at me to get out of her kitchen. She says she's sick and tired of me always in the way. But I'm good in the kitchen. I clean the place up better than she does. You ought to hear how nasty she gets with me. She makes me so mad I clam up before I say something to her I'll regret. Then she gets mad at me for shutting up. You can't win with this woman. It seems everything I do to help out irritates her.

When I think of how good we had it all those years growing up together and now it's come to this. When we should be enjoying ourselves, she's moping around the house all day. At least once or twice a week she leaves the house early in the morning with a friend and doesn't come home until dinnertime.

I ask her where in the hell she's been all day and why she didn't tell me when she'd be home. I tell her to be sure to keep her cellphone on, but she always says she forgot and that's all I get out of her. Once I caught her sneaking packages in from the car. I hate it when she doesn't tell me what she's doing. Don't get me wrong. She can go anywhere she wants anytime and buy whatever she needs. I just want a little common courtesy from her. She acts like it's none of my business. Why can't she be more like she was when we got married?

– LESSON TWO –
We Choose All Our Behavior

Almost every husband or wife that we have asked the question whose behavior can you control, answers, "**I never start it, but she makes me upset and angry. What else can I do?**"

In this lesson, you will learn the choice theory answer to the question "Who can you control?"

Both of you can choose to replace the external control you are choosing now with a much more effective behavior, **choice theory**. Since you already have been introduced to external control, what you will learn in this chapter is deceptively simple: each of us chooses all we do. That means that as much as you choose to use a great deal of external control behavior it is still a choice and a better choice is always possible. The choice we offer here and throughout the rest of this book is to replace the external control you are using now with choice theory. To begin, we want to introduce you to the following choice theory axiom: **All we do from birth to death is behave, and every behavior is chosen.**

Without exception, this means that every thought that comes into your head and every physical action, including the expression on your face, the gestures you make with your hands, and every tone and inflection in your voice, is a choice. When your wife criticized you, she chose to do it. When you started to argue with her in return, you chose to do it. She could have chosen not to criticize and you could have chosen not to argue with her. Although it didn't feel like a choice—no one can make you do anything—you both chose to do what you did, and you both believed that what you did was right.

Tom, and especially Janet, both believe that the other's behavior is controlling them. The fact is no one can control you unless you choose to let them. Choice theory explains what was actually going on between them. They need to learn that they can replace the external control they are both currently using, which is so harmful to their relationship, with choice theory. This theory explains in great detail how to get along much better with your marital partner, but we strongly suggest that you also use it in every one of your important relationships in life.

Choice theory is made up of four major components. We will explain each of the four components in this and the next three lessons. Here we will start with the first component: the **Five Basic Needs.** We call these needs basic because they are encoded in our genetic structure. Every behavior we choose from birth to death is motivated by one or more of these five needs. When we satisfy a need, we feel pleasure. When we try and fail to satisfy a need, we feel pain.

We start learning to satisfy our needs when we are born by crying, which lets our mother know we need food, comfort, and love. Later, we will try to learn how to satisfy the rest of our needs. When we succeed, we are generally happy.

The five basic needs are Survival, Love and Belonging, Freedom, Fun, and Power. Survival—essentially food, shelter, and safety, which are readily available for most people in our society—is a need we don't worry much about on an everyday basis. But survival has another important aspect that often leads to marriage because, as all mammals are, we are also genetically motivated to sustain our species' survival by engaging in reproductive behaviors. However, most humans have learned that sex can be enjoyed without procreation.

Although we do not realize it, some of our strongest sexual motivation—for example, infatuation—is driven as much by the need for species survival as by love. We often get tired of the same sexual partner because species survival wants us to spread our genes around as widely as we can.

Love combined with belonging are not only human needs but are present in other mammals as well. All species are genetically driven to procreate and care for offspring. But in humans, love and belonging can last a lifetime, as we learn to enjoy family love and also the deep friendships associated with belonging. Basically we need each other; relationships are driven by the need for love and belonging, but we would get along with each other better if we did not have the other needs, for example, freedom, fun, and, especially, power. Tom and Janet probably love each other, but that love is constantly being challenged by their needs for freedom and especially power. It is this need for power that causes so much friction in Tom and Janet's marriage.

Freedom is an easier need for other mammals to satisfy than it is for us because very few other mammals develop the long-term marital ties and family obligations we do. Janet struggles, unsatisfactorily but she gets her need for freedom met by escaping a couple of times a week for an all-day outing only to return at the end of the day to the controlling eyes of Tom.

Lasting marital ties tend to be stronger in women than in men because traditionally women have been more involved in child care than men. We think the evidence to support that conclusion is valid: More men than women walk away from their mates and children. The evidence is apparent in Janet's staying with Tom all these years, even though their children are grown.

Fun, which we believe is the enjoyment of learning something useful, sometimes takes us away from our mates and family. But fun can also be strongly tied to family relationships because whole families can participate in learning, both as spectators and as participants. So, although fun can be divisive—as is easily seen in the fierce battles between husband and wife at the bridge table—we believe fun is generally marriage- and family-friendly.

Power is a uniquely human need. Animals may fight at mating time to pass along their genes; they may kill to eat or to defend a territory. But they do not fight over the belief that they are right and others are wrong, as we do and as Tom and Janet consistently do. Except for survival, they are having trouble satisfying all of their needs, especially their need for power. They have yet to learn how to satisfy their need for power without taking power away from each other. Since they are set in their ways after so many years of marriage, it is unlikely that this problem will ever be solved. Unless one or the other learns what we will now explain, their marriage will limp along like this forever. Driven by power, countless couples extend external control into every part of their lives.

They are engaged in daily marital combat because war is a uniquely human endeavor. We killed over a billion people in hostilities during the twentieth century, and we are off to a roaring start in this century.

Since you and your mate are reading this book to learn to get along better with each other, you are already aware that **external control is not in your genes—it is a chosen behavior not a need.** You don't have to use it in your marriage. While this behavior is derived from our need for power, **it is learned.** Even though almost all the people in the world use it when they are having difficulties with other people doesn't mean that married couples can't learn a choice theory behavior to replace their use of external control.

The basic needs have a lot to do with marital compatibility. For example, couples who share a high need for love and a low need for power tend to be happier together. Couples who share a high need for power and a low need for love will spend a lot of their time bickering about who is in charge and who is right. Like Tom and Janet, they are not compatible in the long run but were very attracted to each other in the beginning of their relationship. The old adage "opposites attract" is good for infatuation and great for procreation, but it's disastrous for marriage.

We have taught a lot of people what we are trying to teach you in this book, and they are much happier than they were before they learned it. We advise you and your partner to do more than read these lessons. Go over them very carefully and think about how you might use each lesson in your relationship.

Since you can control only your own behavior and since all your behavior is motivated by your needs, the question this lesson asks you to discuss with each other is **How compatible is the way you are attempting to satisfy your basic needs with the way your partner is choosing to get his or her needs met?**

ON THE EDGE with Earl, Nadine & Weederman

BY JOE MARTIN & DR. JON CARLSON

"MY HUSBAND THRIVES ON PUTTING PEOPLE DOWN. HIS FAVORITE SAYING IS, 'ANYBODY CAN DO THAT!'"

As Bern Williams said, "A friend is a lot of things, but a critic he isn't." He should remember, "Don't belittle, be big", and help others to feel competent. You might try getting him a Don Rickles album and see if he doesn't recognize himself.

Dan and Karen's Story

My name is Karen, and I'm married to the biggest put-down artist on the face of the earth. Before we got married, Dan and I were so in love we'd write poetry to each other. I mention this because the way we relate to each other now is just the opposite of how we did then. I always knew Dan was a kidder—you know, constantly playing pranks on people—but I never took him seriously. I thought he was real funny then, but now his routine has gotten very old and extremely stale.

Dan is such a baby. Whenever anything goes wrong in his life, even something simple, like when he tanked his golf game the other day, he comes home all crabby and takes it out on me. He complains that it's my fault. He says I made him stay up too late visiting friends the night before, so for whatever reason, his failure is always my fault.

His put-downs are constant and never-ending. It's as if he needs to make fun of me in order to feel better about himself. All I know is I'm fed up with his sulking and cutting remarks. By the end of the day I'm so turned off by his negativity I can't wait to go to sleep, but he insists on sex, which I do to get it over with. While we're doing it, he never says one word. Once when we were driving to our annual boring vacation, he didn't say a word to me during the whole two-day trip there.

I have a sneaking suspicion he is having an affair. He gets phone calls on his cell and goes outside to talk. If that's what's really happening here, we're through. I won't tolerate infidelity.

I just don't get it. He's changed so much from the way we were, but on occasion, when we do exchange a few serious words, he won't admit there's anything wrong. He just makes fun of me by saying I take things too seriously. Why don't I just lighten up? I would, but the things he says trying to be funny really hurt my feelings. When I tell him how he hurt me, he always says he was just kidding. Sometimes he doesn't say anything. He just starts to laugh at me, so I wonder what I just did that he's making fun of now. I wish we could go back to the way we were or somehow find out what went wrong.

※

I'm Karen's husband, Dan. I kid a lot, that's just the way I am. Before we got married, she liked it. I'm the same as I always was, but now everything I say offends her. She's totally lost her sense of humor. She bristles anytime I try to have any fun. She's constantly scolding me like a child, telling me how I offended her or somebody else. She's turned into a real wet blanket. We used to have a lot of fun. Anything I wanted to do, she was always up for it. She used to be very enthusiastic about my interests.

When we first got married, we used to go on golf outings. She seemed to look forward to them. Now she says it's boring. We still go, and to really nice places, but are they good enough for her? No way. I guess she wants something more. I'll be damned if I know what it is. She never says what she wants to do. I guess she expects me to read her mind. I hate that.

She gets mad at me all the time, and half the time I don't even know what I did. Then she gives me the cold shoulder and ignores me for days. I'm telling you, I'm sick of her moodiness. It's like she's on a constant PMS roller coaster. I never know from one day to the next what's going to set her off. Life with her is like walking on eggs.

I feel like she's always finding fault with me, so lately I've been just keeping my mouth shut around her. Then I get in trouble for not talking. I swear there's no pleasing this woman except in bed. She still likes having sex with me, or at least she never says no, unless I've been a bad boy according to her. She doesn't keep that a secret. I can read it all over her face.

Sometimes I just wish she would make an effort to understand me more. I'm not that complicated. All I want to do is have a couple of laughs. What's so wrong about that? She acts like I've committed a crime if I tease anybody. I just wish she'd lighten up and get off my back. We could have a lot of fun together, like we used to, if she'd just accept me the way I am.

– LESSON THREE –
Never Use the Seven Deadly Habits

The seven deadly habits are the external control behaviors you and your spouse have been using more and more as your marriage has continued downhill. The first and we believe deadliest habit is **criticism**. Listen to your arguments, and you will hear how full of criticism they are. Comedy routines about marriage are symphonic in their orchestration of this habit.

After criticism comes **blaming**. The marital dialogues between unhappy couples are filled with blame. It is never the blaming partner's fault; it is always the other's fault. Commonly, one partner criticizes, the other blames, and they both **complain**. Don and Karen have mastered all of these habits and more. Whenever you make fun of someone, it is always perceived as criticism and can escalate into an argument.

Then, if the argument continues, one partner will start to **nag**; the other will start to **threaten**, which will lead to **punishing** and then to **bribing.** In one argument it is common for all the deadly habits to make an appearance. Obviously, there are more than seven, but if you can get the following seven: criticizing, blaming, complaining, nagging, threatening, punishing, and bribing out of all your marital interactions, your marriage will improve significantly.

If Don and Karen, who are both well acquainted with the seven deadly habits, want to improve their relationship, they might well ask, if we can't use those, what should we do instead? To replace the deadly habits, there are seven caring habits of choice theory.

The first is **supporting.** When you are supportive of your partner, you say things like, "Honey, don't be so hard on yourself. So you made a little mistake. We can live with it. Let's stick together and find a solution. Okay?" Couples who support each other through the hard times build a relationship that can last a lifetime. Always remember you have each other.

The next caring habit is **encouraging.** You feel encouraged by your partner when you hear words of praise like, "You sure did a great job!" You become each other's cheerleaders. You let your spouse know you are behind him or her every step of the way. Couples who are encouraging of each other have a confidence that helps them succeed in every aspect of their lives.

Listening is the third caring habit. Of all the caring habits, listening is the most asked for and least given. If you want to help each other feel that your power need is being met, listen to each other without evaluating what you hear. Listen carefully to what your partner says and try to truly understand by asking questions such as, "Could you give me more information to help me know what you want me to hear?" You may not always agree with what you have heard, but if you both feel listened to, it brings you closer together.

The fourth habit is **accepting**. When your partner finally sees the real you, which sometimes is not a pretty sight, but nevertheless he or she says, "I love you just the way you are right now." In a relationship, that is the essence of acceptance. You accept each other's imperfections and trust that you are each doing the best you can at the time. We all have our sterling moments when we shine. Recognize those in each other, just as you accept the fact that nobody's perfect, and you will be adding the cement that bonds you together.

The fifth caring habit is **trusting.** This is a big one. Trusting someone else is never easy. We have all trusted someone in our life and had that trust broken, felt rejected, betrayed, and hurt. In marriage, trust is like commitment: It is the heart and soul of love. Showing your partner that you are trustworthy is the best way to gain trust. Tell each other the truth whenever you can do so without hurting your partner. Tell each other you trust each other, because without that knowledge you are all alone. Trust unites a loving couple.

The caring habit that is missing most in unhappy marriages is **respecting**. In the story you would write about your marriage, where would you rank mutual respect? A lot has been written about self-esteem, but we are talking about spouse esteem. Find the things that you really respect in each other and focus on them. Tell your partner what you respect about him or her. If you have respect, you would always act with respect. If you lose respect, you lose everything.

There is also a seventh extremely important caring habit: **negotiating differences**. Differences will surface in the best of marriages. When you negotiate, you give up something to get something. This is not bribing. When you negotiate, you both give and get honestly. It's like buying a home. The owner wants two hundred thousand dollars, and you offer one hundred fifty thousand. He comes down twenty-five thousand. You go up twenty-five thousand. You have a deal at one hundred seventy-five thousand.

If either party in the negotiation is inflexible, it won't work. You may want to add **inflexibility** to the deadly habits. An inflexible stance may have caused much of your trouble in the first place.

But when you use the caring habits, you have to be very careful not to introduce external control into the negotiation. For example, you read this lesson and tell your partner that you really believe criticizing is harming your marriage. Your partner agrees and asks **What are you going to do?** You tell her that you are going to stop criticizing. Your partner then says something like, **"I suppose you expect me to stop criticizing, too?"**

That sounds fair or at least reasonable, but you need to be very careful here. If you want to stay on the choice theory track, you say, "I believe criticizing is bad for our marriage, and **I'm going to stop whether you stop or not**. I can choose to control my own behavior, but I will not attempt to control yours. I think we can have a better marriage if I don't tell you what to do."

This is also a negotiation, but it is a special kind of choice theory negotiation. Choice theory teaches that in a dispute you could easily give a little for a while whether you get anything in return or not. It's like throwing a little bread on the water when you're fishing.

If you can learn to negotiate this way, you can clearly spotlight the difference between choice theory and external control, especially if both partners learn to give rather than demand. If you make it a point to surprise your partner with this kind of giving negotiation once in a while in your marriage, you will both actually feel how much more friendly this use of choice theory is than external control.

External control may feel right at the time Don and Karen use it, but it plays havoc with their happiness. Remember, you are genetically programmed to get your need for love and belonging met. When you do anything to push someone you need away, you suffer. If Don and Karen or any couple can start to use these caring habits with no sarcasm entering into their conversations, they will have started to turn their marriage around.

The question for you both to discuss for this lesson is **Which of the caring habits do we need to work on first in order to get along better?**

ON THE EDGE with Earl, Nadine & Weederman

BY JOE MARTIN & DR. JON CARLSON

A BIG PART OF THE REASON MAGICIANS AREN'T ALLOWED IN THE O.B. WARDS

"I THINK HAVING A BABY IS A PRIVATE AFFAIR, BUT MY HUSBAND WANTS TO MAKE A BIG PRODUCTION OF IT - LIKE HE'S SPIELBERG!"

Fact: Boundaries and privacy are important in families. The Irish proverb states, "The three most beautiful sights: a potato garden in bloom, a ship in sail, a woman after the birth of her child." This is a moment to experience and not to memorialize. Tell him you really want him to participate in the delivery, but only if he can get through the metal detector.

Mark and Rachel's Story

More than anything else in the whole world I want to start a family. I've wanted a baby since I turned thirty. I guess my biological clock, as they say, has been ticking loud and clear for the last five years. Mark says we have plenty of time to think about that. We've been married now for seven years, and I think it's time. I don't want to wait any longer.

We have a little starter house with manageable payments so that I could quit my job and we could still make it on Mark's salary. Things might be a little tight at first until Mark gets his promotion, but I'm convinced we can do this. The only problem is Mark doesn't see it my way. He wants to wait another year before we even discuss it.

Whenever we go out and see other couples who have children I get so jealous it wrecks my whole evening. Mark says what's wrong with you, and I have one answer for him—baby lust. I really don't think I can take this much longer. I'm obsessed with it. It's all I think about day and night. I go shopping at the mall and I'm drawn to the baby merchandise featuring baby clothes and baby paraphernalia. It's all so cute that I want to buy everything I see.

I daydream about what I would call the baby. I even secretly bought a book of names. If it's a girl, I'll call her Juliet or Elizabeth after my grandmother. If it's a boy, I'd like to call him Trevor, simply because I like the name.

I get angry at Mark sometimes because he's so stubborn. He knows how much I want this baby. Why won't he give me this one thing? It's all I ask. I tell him I'm begging him to change his mind, and he always says, Rachel, don't start in on that again. So here I am playing a waiting game. It hurts me to think he cares so little about what I want. We've been so happy together, but this is starting to affect our relationship. I love being married to Mark, but if I can't get him to do this, I don't know what I'm going to do. We see this so differently. I wish I could tell him how deeply I feel about this. But whenever I try to, he shuts me out. I would love to convince him to start a family now before I get too old.

It's easy for a man. They can start a family anytime, but it's different for me. I can't let this go and every day the feeling just gets stronger. I'm so frustrated because I want Mark to share this with me, and it hurts me to put pressure on him.

❊

Rachel is driving me crazy. She never lets up. Lately, it's baby this and baby that until our ability to converse about anything without turning to the baby topic is impossible. Don't get me wrong. I want a family someday but not right now. She keeps saying, Mark, c'mon why not? Please. I've given her a lot of good reasons. Mainly, I'm just not ready to be strapped down with that kind of responsibility yet. We're still young. We have the freedom to go everywhere and do anything. Besides, I'd like to save a little more of a nest egg before she quits her job. She says she'd go back to work, but I know Rachel. Once that baby's here, I'm afraid she's home to stay.

I wouldn't mind if she stays home with the baby when we can afford it better. We have a mortgage to pay, and my big promotion hasn't come through yet. When it does, and I'm sure it will, I'll be more than willing to discuss it. She thinks I just don't care enough about her to give her what she wants. But that's not fair. I do care about her. I wouldn't be so careful if I didn't care about my family's welfare, including the child's. She knows I want to be a good father someday. We talked about that even before we got married.

But she doesn't seem to recognize what I need. It seems like she cares more about having a baby than she cares about me. I'm beginning to resent that, and I know she resents me. One night she even called me a selfish prick. She's never said anything like that to me before. We've been so happy together. I'm worried that the kid is going to come between us. Up until now I've come first with her. I'm sure that'll change when the baby comes. Now I am sounding like a selfish prick.

It looks like what I want and what she's willing to accept are at opposite ends of the spectrum, and I don't know how to fix it. All I want is some more time. Why can't she see that?

– LESSON FOUR –

Get Acquainted
with Each Other's Quality World

To understand what has been happening in your brain since your marriage began going downhill, we must explain the next choice theory concept—the **Quality World.** If you remember that in the beginning of this book, we said what we were going to teach you could save your marriage if there is some semblance of love left in it. When we said that, we were hoping that both of you still had a small picture of each other in your quality worlds, a picture that would not be there if you didn't care for each other. People are a very important component of our Quality World, and we depict them as need-satisfying pictures.

Let us explain. In our brains, where all our knowledge is

stored, we create a small simulation of the world we would most like to live in. It is called the Quality World. We start creating this unique world soon after birth, and we keep creating and moving pictures in and out of it for the rest of our lives. This world, **created from our most pleasurable experiences**, is made up of pictures of the people we most enjoy, the images of the things we get great pleasure from, and the systems of belief that govern our lives.

We need to understand that it is neither a moral world nor a diet and exercise world. It is a feel-good world created from our own most pleasurable feelings, but because it is created out of pleasure, it can be very destructive to our marriage. Relatively small pictures of things in your Quality World can become huge in your marriage, especially if you don't understand exactly what they are.

For example, your husband is not an alcoholic, but he likes one or two glasses of good wine with dinner every evening. Drinking those two glasses are now very important pictures in his Quality World. You don't even like wine in the house much less on the dinner table, and you keep bickering with him about the wine. The deadly habits are alive and well in your marriage over the wine.

With this example we are trying to explain the impact that your very different Quality Worlds can have on the compatibility of your marriage. We imagine that after years of an unhappy marriage, there are many Quality World differences between you and your partner. The only way you can deal with

them successfully is to use the caring habits, especially, to negotiate differences. In Mark and Rachel's dilemma, they are
still in each other's Quality World, but they have very different
pictures that are causing strife.

The only way any of us, including Mark and Rachel, can
change a Quality World picture is to replace it with a more
need-satisfying picture. For Rachel this would be extremely difficult because her genes are driving her to have a baby. If Mark
could put a picture of himself as a happily married father in
his Quality World right now, all the strife would be resolved. If
he won't do this, it could become a turning point in their marriage. If they can't negotiate this difference, they may never be
happy. If they can learn how important each other's Quality
World pictures are, they have a chance to overcome their problem. They need to talk to each other about the incompatible
pictures in their Quality Worlds and try to decide what each
would be willing to change.

In the case of the couple with the wine problem, they will
have to decide together if the most important picture in both of
their Quality Worlds, **the picture of them being happily married to each other,** can take precedence over what each individual wants. If they agree that it can, then they would negotiate
for less wine. But they need to be careful not to try to negotiate
for no wine—that will never fly.

Look at the bright side. You have been unhappy about your
marriage for quite a while, but you have agreed to read this
book together. If you can put the information we explain in

these lessons into both of your Quality Worlds, you will have a much better marriage. Let's continue by taking a more detailed look at the Quality World.

The first pictures we put into our Quality World are of people we love and enjoy being with. For many of us, the first picture we put in is our mother. We will keep her there even after she's gone as a very pleasant memory. Then there are other early pictures of fathers, aunts, uncles, brothers and sisters, our children and grandchildren.

Another very important part of the Quality World is our long-term good friends because what makes them good friends is that they rarely try to control us. We never keep anyone who tries to control us in our Quality World, but we make a special exception for close family members, such as parents and occasionally grandparents. But even they are not sacrosanct. If they get too controlling, we will take them out or place them in a dark, obscure corner, out of sight and out of earshot.

For the most part, the people we put into our Quality World are people who think and act very much as we do. But there is a sexual trap you should be aware of. Opposites are often strongly sexually attracted to each other, but this attraction is based on the external control assumption: **With my love, he or she will change and become the person I want in my Quality World.** If that assumption is carried into a marriage, that marriage is almost never happy.

But those marriages seldom occur because one or both partners are using love to attempt to control the other, and that control soon destroys the initial attraction. When celebrities, who believe the world should make a special exception for them, get married and then quickly divorce, this is often what has happened. As soon as one or the other refuses to change to what they each want from the other, there is no longer any reason to stay married. These marriages are like geese that lay golden eggs for divorce attorneys.

Keep in mind that we tolerate more external control from family members in our Quality World because we are genetically related to our mother, father, and the rest of the family. But that genetic toleration does not extend to the people we marry. Our initial attraction is sexual, and when that feeling wanes, as it will, there is no genetic link to keep that person in our Quality World. The only way to keep our partners in our Quality World is to create a relationship that is need-satisfying to both.

We tolerate a great deal of external control from people we need for survival, such as our boss, because the boss is our bread and butter. Students put great teachers, never controlling teachers, into their Quality Worlds. An unrealistic number of students, mostly males who have completely normal brains, refuse to pay attention in school because they are taught in a very controlling system they really don't like.

Too many are then diagnosed as ADHD and prescribed strong brain-altering drugs such as Ritalin, the long-term effects of which are just now being discovered. These same boys will grow up someday and become the husbands and fathers whose marital problems we will all need to address. Teaching them choice theory now could help them find the happiness they need to become good partners in the future.

This is a major problem in most schools that could be easily and inexpensively corrected by teaching teachers to use choice theory. In the schools where they use this theory, there is no manifestation of ADHD diagnoses. The students are happy, work hard, and are successful. The teachers also have happier marriages than most teachers, which we consider to be one of the residual benefits of learning choice theory.

Things or objects make up a less important part of our Quality World than people, but as in the previous example of the wine, they can become very important. Mostly the Quality World contains things such as your prized possessions or even things that are important to you that you do not own, such as a beautiful beach or a wonderful museum.

But here we run head-on into an important subject: compatibility. If one partner places her home into her Quality World and works to decorate it beautifully and keep it spotless and the other is a slob, as in Neil Simon's play *The Odd Couple*, their marriage is severely challenged. Since compatibility depends on couples sharing major parts of their Quality Worlds, it would be wise to take some time to talk over your possession incompatibilities with your partner. If you can adjust them, it's usually well worth doing.

Addictions in one or both partners, Quality Worlds are another class of behaviors and things that are usually disastrous to a marriage. Addictive drugs like alcohol and tobacco and addictive behaviors like gambling can destroy a marriage.

Problems of addiction usually require professional help. The partners can't help each other, but they can talk the problem over, make the decision to seek help, and support each other while one or both are getting the help.

Addictions are complicated and beyond the scope of this book. But it should be obvious that since so many addicts are unhappily married, learning to get along well together is the best treatment plan for any addictive behavior. Good relationships help the recovering addict stay in recovery and avoid relapse.

The third component of your Quality World is systems of belief. If your religious or political beliefs are very different, you will have trouble. If your beliefs about how you spend your money are incompatible, you are looking for trouble. But if you can keep each other in your Quality Worlds by reading this book, you may be able to work these differences out by talking them over, with neither of you forcing the other to change.

You are reading this book together to try to find out that there is more for you to do than remove external control from your marriage. You are also trying to find out if there are enough positive qualities in your relationship to build the Quality World you need to be happily married. But if you think you can reclaim the early infatuation once it is over, you will be disappointed. But, on the bright side, you could create something far better and longer lasting. You can also reexamine your own Quality World and perhaps find each other somewhere inside it. Then build on that small picture by adding new happy experiences you can share together.

The question you can talk about before going on to the next lesson is **What do you need to negotiate to make your Quality Worlds more compatible?**

DO I REALLY NEED ALL THESE PILLS?

There's a good chance you don't. Many believe if one pill is good, two must be twice as good! 15 million (and growing) are addicted to prescription drugs! Check with your physician, and another one, about what you are taking.

Ron and Beverly's Story

My wife, Beverly, is a flaming hypochondriac. You name it, she's got it. Not a day goes by that she isn't complaining that one thing or another hurts her. Whenever we watch television, one ad after another is about asking your doctor for drugs to treat diseases I've never even heard of. But, sure enough, the next day Beverly knows she has it. She's making me sick just listening to her complaints.

The worst thing of all is she uses these symptoms whenever she doesn't want to do anything I want to do. Like sex, for instance—it's always something. She outclasses the classical "Honey I can't. I have a headache."

Take our last vacation, for example. She ruined it for everyone. We went on a dream cruise with another couple, people we actually like. She spent the bulk of the time in our cabin seasick, even when we were anchored in port. I had to go to everything without her. I mean she apologized to everybody and we all felt sorry for her. She missed a really good cruise. I just wish we could find out what's wrong with her. I don't believe she's actually sick, but if I even hint at that, she becomes furious.

I don't know what to do with her. I try to be sympathetic, but that seems to make things worse. She goes to every doctor in town, but they never seem to be able to find anything wrong with her. One of them told her to see a therapist. She was so insulted she never went back to him.

You may wonder why I stay with her, but she is really a beautiful woman who with all her complaints pays a lot of attention to her appearance. The truth is I'm still powerfully attracted to her, and once in a while when she's in the mood, we have great sex. I keep hoping she'll start to focus more on how much I love her instead of always thinking she's sick or about to get sick.

I don't know what she wants out of life, but she never seems to be satisfied. She has a job that she's good at, but it doesn't seem to be enough to make her happy. I tell her that with her education she could work anywhere, but the people she works for now put up with her frequent sick days because somehow she always gets her work done and what she does is very competent. I have to say she's pretty much of a perfection-ist. Maybe that's what's wearing her out. She tries too hard. I wish she'd put that much effort into us.

I'm Beverly and I'm married to Ron. He thinks he's Mr. Per-sonality, good-time Charley. He acts like he's so incredibly in-terested in everybody's life, but his main interest in life is himself. His goal seems to be getting everyone to think he's the friend they've been avidly searching for and finally found.

Ron is like the straw man in the *Wizard of Oz*. There is simply no substance to him, and he has zero awareness of the way he is. All he cares about are appearances. If I look good, it's good enough for him. Well, sometimes I just don't feel good, and he seems unable to understand that. All he cares about is his own gratification. People all exist for his pleasure.

I try to look my best all the time, even when I don't feel like it. As sick as I am sometimes, I can always hide it with makeup. I go to work. I come home. I try to be a good wife to a man who hasn't a clue as to what I need to give my life meaning.

I feel like no matter how hard I try, I'm not getting anywhere. My job is a dead end, but Ron says if I don't like it I should find something else to do. He's probably right. He acts like he cares, but I know he's just treating me like he treats everyone else, with faux concern. If he really cared, he wouldn't pay so much attention to everyone and everything else. He would act like my life was important to him. He would listen to me.

Once in a while he does and that really turns me on. When he makes love to me, I feel that's the only time I merit his esteem. I guess on some level I know he loves me in his own superficial way, and I love him. That's what keeps us together. I just wish I could feel happier. I wish we could be more.

– LESSON FIVE –
Understand Total Behavior

So far you have learned the difference between external control and choice theory. You have also learned about your basic needs and your Quality World. We believe you are ready to learn another component of choice theory, **Total Behavior.** This is a short easy-to-explain component. If you make the effort to understand it, you will be able to put it to work in your marriage. Knowing the concept of Total Behavior will help you learn how to relate to each other in more satisfying ways.

Ron and Beverly have a very unhappy marriage. All they tend to think about are their feelings, both physical and emotional. The unhappier their marriage became, the more they complained to each other and anyone else who would listen to their misery. The problem with those complaints is, after a short period of time, no one really listens. Increasingly, they both began to believe that no one cares, especially their partners.

The sad truth about all these complaints and the miserable feelings that go with them is, as they continue, people care less and less. People will even tell you that if you're so upset, why don't you do something about it? But you don't know what to do. You don't know that focusing so much on your own feelings is harmful to your marriage. Ron and Beverly could learn to focus on their **acting and thinking** and choose to act and think in ways that help them feel better.

What we will teach in this lesson that could help Ron and Beverly is that all **behavior is Total Behavior.** For example, what you are both doing right now, reading this book is a Total Behavior called reading. That Total Behavior is made up of four separate parts: **thinking, acting, feeling, and physiology.**

As you read, you are **thinking** about what you're reading. At the same time you are **acting** by following the sentences across and down the page with your eyes. If you enjoy what you are reading, you may **feel** so good that you get excited, your heart rate increases, and this gets your **physiology** involved. These four components all occur at the same time; that's why they are called Total Behavior.

If you were reading something you couldn't relate to, you'd **think** Why am I reading this book? You might **act** by paying little attention to what you are reading. You might feel unhappy, be bored out of your mind, and doze off. When you do, your **physiology** becomes involved and your heart rate and breathing slow down.

What is important to know about Total Behavior is you only have **voluntary control** over your **thinking** and your **acting**. If you are **feeling** bad and complaining about it all the time, like Ron and Beverly, you will continue to feel the same or worse because you have no direct control over your **feelings** or your **physiology.** You have no way to improve your marriage unless you and your partner both **think** and **act** to replace the external control you are using now with choice theory.

Think of yourselves as two four-wheel-drive cars on a busy highway. The motor is the basic needs. The steering wheel controls the front wheels, which are **acting and thinking**. The rear wheels, which also move the car, are **feeling and physiology,** but they have to follow the front wheels. If you are in an unhappy marriage and using a lot of external control, the front wheels, acting and thinking, are taking you in the direction of trying to control your partner. If you can't succeed in controlling your partner or getting what you want, you then **feel** unhappy, possibly even sick, as the rear wheels follow miserably along.

Beverly is trying to be perfect, and she is actually making herself sick in the process because she'll never succeed. No one can be perfect. She blames Ron, who is also far from perfect in her eyes, instead of figuring out how to think about her life and their life together and act to do something about it.

If you want to feel better and have a healthier physiology, you can steer the front wheels, **thinking and acting**, toward a choice theory marriage. Since the rear wheels have to follow the front wheels, you will **feel** better and your **physiology** will be healthier.

When you are unhappy for a long time, as you and your partner have been, what you may have done is turn the car around and lead with your rear wheels. You are then trying to feel better with no effective control over your thinking and acting. With such reckless driving, you'll very likely get into an accident. For both of you, your unhappy marriage is the ongoing accident.

This is what you do when you get involved in an addiction. You drink or gamble to feel better with no concern for how disastrous your addiction is to the relationships you cherish, and your life careens out of control.

In a happy marriage in which you understand Total Behavior, as soon as you feel unhappy, you will say to each other, "We have to stop focusing on how badly we feel and start changing the way we're thinking and acting." You can remind each other of the car and offer to help each other steer in a more satisfying direction.

This may sound too simple for you to believe when you are this unhappy, but it works. Think of your marriage as stuck in the mud because you have skidded off the road. If you try to get out by spinning your rear wheels, you will get no traction and dig yourselves deeper in the mud. You need to help each other to get out of the rut by digging yourselves out with more effective thoughts and actions and then carefully steering your lives on to a safe choice-theory road.

In Ron and Beverly's case, we see them both focusing on Beverly's physiology and their negative feelings about each other. It would be wise for them to talk about this and see if they could spend more time doing activities they both enjoy. They need to find ways to laugh and play together to take their minds off how bad they feel. This may seem easy for us to say and very hard for you to do when you're stuck in the mud. Yet there is nothing easy about a miserable marriage.

Beverly's rear wheels are in control of their marriage, and Ron's rear wheels are following right along. Neither of them has been using front-wheel behaviors. Read this chapter over and picture how your own behavioral car is affecting your marriage. Remember, it's your choice in which direction to steer your marriage. Think about how you can focus on your thinking and acting, not your feelings and physiology.

We suggest that you think of something new to do together. You can create a plan to make your marriage better. The idea is to get moving. Do something, anything—just have some fun together.

This is a short but very important lesson. Many unhappily married people get stuck in the seven deadly habits of external control with all their miserable feelings. They don't realize that they can get their marriage back on track with choice theory.

The key to the car analogy is to always move forward. Keep your eyes on the road ahead. Occasionally, look in your rearview mirror to see what's behind you, but don't dwell on an unhappy past too long. This can cause a serious accident, full of resentment and revenge. Stay focused on what you can do on the road ahead.

Your assignment for this lesson is to discuss with each other what you have just read and then answer this question honestly: **Which wheels are in control of our marriage—our front wheels or our rear wheels?**

"MY WIFE LOOKS AT THE WORLD THROUGH ROSE-COLORED GLASSES AND SUGARCOATS EVERYTHING. AM I A STICK-IN-THE-MUD?"
A relationship is a lot like a teeter-totter. If your partner is too optimistic, you are probably a stick-in-the-mud. As you get out of the mud, her vision will change. You need to remove the word "NO" from your vocabulary when your wife asks you to do something. Take a walk with her on the sunny side of the street!!

Amanda and Sam's Story

My husband, Sam, is a couch potato. He comes home from work, grabs a Coke, turns on the TV, and hangs out on the couch the rest of the evening. He does this day in and day out, without doing much more than change the station. He's so boring he's eaten the same breakfast every day since before we got married. He is totally predictable twenty-four seven. I could set my watch by his little rituals.

He gets up every morning, brings in the paper, and eats his cereal with one hand while reading the paper, holding it up exactly the same way with the other hand. He never voices an opinion about what he's reading. He just reads as if all the parts of the paper are the same.

He never consults me if we're going out somewhere, but he just plans it as if it's what I want to do and expects me to like it. If I ever suggest anything, he'll listen and then say not today but maybe next time. He is not what you would call flexible or innovative.

I tell him I'm bored all the time, but he keeps saying, what do you want from me? He says I'm always blaming him for being bored, so why don't I do something about it. I tell him I want him to do something with me that I want to do. He says, what's that? And I honestly don't know. I can't think of anything I'd want to do with him.

Well, maybe one thing. I'd like us to take ballroom dancing lessons, but my chances of getting him to do that are slim to nonexistent. I don't even bother to ask. I know he wouldn't do it anyway.

We have a stepdaughter from his first marriage. She's okay for a teenager, not as difficult to handle as some are. I just wish Sam would take more of an interest in her. She's desperate for his attention, but he just defers his responsibility for her to me. This bugs me because I feel sorry for her. I'm trying to not let her make trouble between us, but I'd like a little more cooperation from him.

My friends tell me he's a good man and I should appreciate the fact that he never complains about our life. He also doesn't drink, smoke, or gamble, he's a good provider, and he certainly doesn't run around on me. He does like to travel on our vacations, and he plans what we do to the last letter. That could be one of the high points of our marriage. Fortunately, he does have a month's vacation every year, and he's willing to spend money to see interesting places. But then it's back home again to the same old boring routine.

I just wish he'd be more exciting, but my friends tell me that an exciting man isn't always a good man to be married to, at least that's been their experience. Good old Sam. I guess I'm stuck with the way he is. He'll never change.

My wife, Amanda, is my second marriage. I still can't figure out why my first wife divorced me, but Amanda is the wife I always wanted. She has taken my daughter from my first marriage in and given her a real home. I know this is hard on my wife and sometimes, being a teenager, my daughter comes between us. She's always trying to get me to take her side whenever she has a problem with Amanda. I just ignore her. I don't know what else to do. Amanda is pretty patient with her. Don't get me wrong. She has her flaws, but she's no wacky accident-waiting-to-happen runaround that my first wife was.

Amanda is pretty patient with me, I have to admit. That's what I liked about her from the get-go. I come home from work tired, and I have my little routines and she lets me be. But here lately she seems to be a little irritated at me. She says she's bored. I don't know why. We go on a nice vacation every year.

The trouble is she doesn't have any interests of her own to keep her busy, like maybe she should take up weaving or pottery. We saw a lot of that on our last vacation, and we have plenty of room in our house for a loom or a pottery wheel and kiln. If she can't find anything that interests her, she's just going to have to stay bored, I guess. It's her problem.

She knew I was no ball of fire when she married me. It's not like I misrepresented myself. She wanted a steady reliable guy like me and she got one. I'll do anything for her within reason. I just hope she can be satisfied. I don't want to lose her.

– LESSON SIX –

A Little Creativity Can Save Your Marriage

W e are all creative. For example, have either of you ever been insulted by someone important to you? You struggled for something clever to say to defend yourself, but nothing came. Hours later, when you thought you had forgotten about the incident, a great retort suddenly popped into your mind. It was too late, but it still felt good. You might even have shared it with someone you know and gotten a compliment for your creativity.

What happened reveals the creativity inherent in everyone's brain. Your brain was working on the insult on its own, trying to come up with something. When it finally did, both you and your brain felt satisfied. Your creativity is unpredictable, but we believe it is always active. It is very active when you sleep by offering you dreams that are so creative they surprise you. I'm a man who has Academy Award–winning dreams.

Several years ago I had a dream I still remember. My car is parked above me and off to the side in a carport when I sleep. That night I dreamed I e-mailed my car into my garage. At that time I didn't even use e-mail, and I've never had a garage. My car is in my Quality World, so in my dream I immediately felt disappointed because when I went into the garage in my dream, my car wasn't there. I did see a small pipe with a cap on it, so I unscrewed the cap and three rusty bolts dropped out. It then came to me that those bolts were all that was left of my car.

When I woke up and went upstairs for the newspaper, I was very happy to see my car in the carport and not lost in cyberspace. I'm sure if we had a dream contest, you could come up with something similar that you still remember.

As counselors, we have listened to the story of many marriages, and it has always surprised us how uncreative most of these marriages are. They are all about how it's my partner's fault, and if he or she would change, the marriage could be so much better. But here, instead of listening to the repetitive boring story of your marriage, we are trying to teach both of you some new behaviors and are urging you to try to put them to work in your marriage in creative ways.

Sam and Amanda are blaming each other for not taking responsibility for their own unhappiness. Sam is unaware of the part he plays in their marriage being at a standstill. Amanda thinks Sam should do something to alleviate her boredom. What both of them do not realize is that neither of them is using any of the creativity latent in their brains and that their marriage will remain that way until one or both of them make the effort to use their creativity.

The most creative thing you can do, which we are sure will surprise your partner, is to say, "I don't think our unhappiness is your fault. I'd like to do something with you to help our marriage come alive that I think you'd enjoy." In our experience, it is amazing how partners approached this way will come up with something they can actually do, like taking a photography class or cooking lessons together. When they use that approach, it makes a big difference, and it's so simple to do.

The problem with Sam and Amanda is that neither is taking any initiative to creatively help their relationship. Sam wants Amanda to take a class by herself when she wants to take ballroom dancing lessons with him. Ballroom dancing may not be of any interest to him, but that doesn't mean they can't put their heads together and come up with something enjoyable that both of them can do together on an ongoing basis besides taking just one vacation a year.

Fun is the genetic reward for learning something new and useful. Times two, it can produce twice the fun and perk up a boring marriage. If Sam and Amanda do this, it may open up their presently closed minds and initiate an enjoyable conversation.

If you and your partner are really bored in your marriage, enjoyable conversations have been few and far between. Then, based on the fact that you can control only your end of the conversation, try very hard not to use any of the deadly habits as you continue to talk about new things to do.

What we are trying to tell you is stop treading on old ground that you have gone over a million times before. We are not saying a new idea to help your marriage need be super-creative, but at least it will be new and supportive. It will take some effort, but any effort to try something new and noncontrolling will nurture your relationship. Whatever you decide to do together, keep in mind that any word or action that removes the deadly habits from your marriage and puts the caring habits into it will make a huge difference to your relationship.

To review, the deadly habits are criticizing, blaming, complaining, nagging, threatening, punishing, and bribing or rewarding to control. Stop using them. Instead, when you embark on your new adventures together, use the caring habits: supporting, encouraging, listening, accepting, trusting, respecting, and negotiating your differences. If you can succeed in doing even a little of this, it will be new to your marriage, and the newness itself will be creative.

Boredom puts sludge into a smooth-running relationship. We don't have many more detailed suggestions, but try to flush boredom out of your married life as often as you can. A good definition of boredom is to behave the same way you always have and expect to get exciting results. Since there is not much courtesy in an unhappy marriage, try our abbreviated version of the golden rule. Treat your partner as he or she would like to be treated, regardless of whether he or she treats you that way. For example, you might start by getting profanity out of your marital vocabulary, or if you are stuffed shirts, put some in.

Don't be predictable. If you are having an argument and your partner makes a good point, suddenly pause and look kindly at him or her, perhaps smile and say, "You know what? I see your point. You're right and I'm wrong." Assuming your partner doesn't have a heart attack, this could be very good for your marriage.

But the big deal is to make an effort to show appreciation for each other. Marriage is tough. There are kids, stepkids, blended families, aging parents, in-laws, pets to be cared for, disagreeable neighbors, and then there is giving money when you can't afford it or borrowing money when you hate to do it. These difficult situations take a lot of work and to fail to give appreciation to the partner who takes on any of these obligations is to miss an important chance to help your marriage.

If Sam could give Amanda some appreciation for what she is doing for his daughter and join her occasionally in her efforts, they would all be better for it. As you talk with each other or with anyone else and your marriage comes up in the conversation, make sure that you refer to your marriage as **our marriage**, not your marriage or my marriage. If anyone asks you why you are behaving differently, tell them you are trying to learn how to act in ways that help your marriage and avoid ways that harm it. If they want to learn more, tell them in as much detail as you both believe you want to share about what you are doing.

Keep laughter alive in your marriage. Watch your favorite comedians, who make light of reality as they see the world in new and funny ways. Take a clue from them. Of course, if you don't like profanity, don't watch comedians who use it. But if your marriage is on the mend, as we hope it is by now, you both need a good laugh. We think marriage is a very serious business, but missing any opportunity to laugh at it by being overserious is a mistake you can learn to correct. Choice theory is a lighthearted psychology. Laughter is good for everyone.

The question to ask yourselves for this lesson is **When is the last time we used our creativity to have a real good time together?**

"MY HUSBAND CARES MORE ABOUT THE DOG THAN ME!"

FACT: In every successful relationship there are five positive responses for every one negative. He must be getting more positives from the dog than you. Take a tip and make it your job to "out-do" the dog each day.

Sarah and Jim's Story

My daughter, Julia, is thirteen years old. Her brother, Matthew, is nine. They are pretty well-adjusted kids. Of course, they have the occasional spat, like any normal brother and sister. But lately my daughter has been very moody and pensive. I've sort of chalked that up to hormones and just everyday teenage girl stuff. Matthew doesn't say much, but I've noticed his grades have not been as good as they ordinarily are.

Yesterday Julia had an outburst. As she was running up the steps to her room and before she slammed the door, she screamed, why can't we be a normal family like everybody else? I was surprised. She must have noticed that Jim and I haven't been getting along. I've been ignoring him lately. We hardly talk anymore except to exchange insults. You can cut the tension in this house with a knife. It's no wonder the kids have sensed something is going on, and they don't like it.

I don't like it either, but I don't know what to do about it. Jim is so irritable all the time, and he takes it out on me. According to him, I can't do anything right. He comes home and starts yelling at us for little things, like Matthew left his bike out in the driveway. Jim grounded him and blamed me for not making him be more responsible. He says I have more time than he does to take care of things. I told him, look, if you're not happy here with the way things are, just let me know. He looked at me like he thought that was a good idea. I felt like saying, there's the door, don't let it hit you on the ass on your way out. I didn't because I was afraid he'd take me up on it. I don't want my children to be from a broken home. I'm just so angry at the way he's been acting lately. Now he's picking on the kids too, and they know we're having problems. You can see it in their eyes.

We don't have our fights in front of them. I've pretty much kept my mouth shut, but there's a time bomb about to go off inside me. But more than anything else I want to keep this family together.

Sarah says things like let's ask Daddy about that. To her I'm not Jim anymore, I'm Daddy. I'm not her father. Whatever happened to Honey or Sweetheart? How did I somehow get trapped in this role? I used to be a pretty cool guy. Women thought I was sexy. I had goals, aspirations, and dreams. Now all I have is a mortgage, a judgmental, irritating mother-in-law who never thought I was good enough for her baby, and a wife who pays more attention to the kids than she does to me.

I work my butt off to keep this family going, and what appreciation do I get? None. All I hear is why can't we get this, we need that, or something is always broken and needs to be fixed. Sarah thinks that because she has a little job, she's doing it all. She doesn't know the kind of pressure I'm under. Some days I don't even want to come home.

I'm not a terrible person or an ogre like she sometimes makes me out to be. I love our kids as much as she does.

They're the reason I stay in this miserable situation. I don't know what happened to us. I loved Sarah when we got married. I guess down deep I still do. But she's going to have to change her attitude, and boy, does she have an attitude.

Our sex life, what's left of it, isn't that great either. We're either too tired or too pissed off at each other to get it on. The fact is I'd like more sex in our life, but with a thirteen-year-old daughter in the house, it's pretty hard to get wild and crazy like we used to. Sometimes at the office I'm tempted to pick something up—it's always out there. I just don't want to risk getting involved in anything and lose my kids.

At Your Discretion, Share What You Are Doing for Your Marriage with Your Children

I f you are looking for ways to improve your marriage by reading this book, consider this. Even though you may both be feeling better about your marriage, your children must be aware of the tension created by the difficulty you had and may still be having with each other. It is certainly possible for you to treat your children in ways that your dissatisfaction does not affect them too much, but they will be a lot happier if you can learn to get along better with each other. Their happiness is a wonderful extra bonus if you are able to help your marriage.

To help you we have created a small skit that clearly explains unhappiness in marriage and what to do about it. If your children are old enough, you can read it to them or with them. They might like to be in it if you act it out with them. There's an actor just beneath the surface in all of us. Lesson Six was about creativity. The following skit is a chance for everyone in the family to be creative by trying their hand at performing this skit.

The skit explains what you are trying to do in language that teenagers or even preteens will understand. Very young children will need some explanation, but we have taught choice theory to five-year-olds and they learn it easily. In fact, if you teach it to a child, you will learn it better yourself and get closer to them at the same time. Read the following skit and see what you think of it. If it seems like something you can use to help your children understand your dilemma and what you can do about it, give it a try.

Pet Peeves

The characters are a Parrot, a Dog, a Cat, and a married couple, Paul and Jan.

You can picture them in your mind's eye or draw a picture of them as you visualize them. Or you could get puppets at a toy store and use them to act out the skit.

Scene One

PARROT: I'll tell you, friends, I'm worried about the folks we live with.

DOG: Gee, Parrot, what's wrong? You hardly ever worry. What about Paul and Jan? What's wrong with them?

PARROT: They keep talking about getting a divorce. If they split up, we could lose our comfortable home.

DOG: But they're so good to us. I don't understand why they can't get along with each other.

CAT: (*Waking up*) Wow, this is serious. I had a good home before this one, and I lost it when my people got a divorce.

PARROT: It's even worse for me. This is my fourth place to live. I'm way too old to start looking for a new one. I've always gotten along well with the people I've lived with, but they all had problems with each other. They'd give it a try for a few years, but after a while they just couldn't get along anymore.

CAT: But we get along great. What they're doing is a big mistake.

PARROT: To me, it's simple—they expect too much from each other. We don't. We leave each other be.

DOG: Live and let live is our motto.

CAT: It sure isn't theirs. In my last home I lived with the wife before she got married, and it was fine. He was around a lot, and they got along so well that I thought for sure it would be that way after they got married. Boy, did they change.

DOG: But that's what's happening here. Don't you remember, Paul and Jan got along okay for a long time, and then they started criticizing each other . . .

CAT: And blaming each other for everything.

PARROT: And complaining about each other. It's been getting worse every year.

DOG: If they'd only treat each other the way they treat us.

CAT: Even in bed, when they could be enjoying a delicious night's sleep, those fools wake up and start arguing with each other. No cat in the world would do such a silly thing.

PARROT: We'll never find another home as good as this one, though. Isn't there anything we can do to help them?

CAT: I try to set a good example. I'm always around, but I never get in the way. They even wake me up to pet me and show me off, and I never complain.

DOG: Cat does set a good example, but it's not enough. If we're ever going to help them, it'll have to be you, Parrot. You speak their language, and being older, you know so much more about people than we do. They'll listen to you.

CAT: You're right about that. Look how excited they get when you say, "Canaries are cute, but they can't talk." They laugh their heads off.

PARROT: I guess I could talk to them, but what would I say?

DOG: You've lived with humans for seventy years. You must have learned something. If I could talk as well as you can, I'd figure out something to say.

CAT: What I've noticed is one of them usually starts the argument, and then they keep bugging each other about it. They never let up.

PARROT: You're right about that. It happens over and over.

CAT: But I've noticed that once in a while one of them stops talking completely. They call that the silent treatment. But while they keep quiet, I love it. My naps are extremely important to me.

DOG: Do you notice how they talk, talk, talk, but they never listen. I'm sure they'd listen to Parrot if he came right out and asked them to.

PARROT: Wouldn't they be surprised if I suddenly screeched "Turn off that TV and listen to us."

DOG: Man, that'd sure get their attention.

CAT: Do you think they'd really listen to us?

DOG: Are you kidding? I think they'd be very curious. If Parrot started talking to them, believe me they'd listen.

CAT: You know, Parrot, if you actually started talking to them, before you know it, you'd get on TV with an agent and everything. You'd make so much money you could buy us our own home.

PARROT: What good would that do? I don't think they're into sharing cash with animals. No way.

CAT: But . . . but Larry King would pay you a fortune if you'd give him an exclusive interview.

PARROT: Calm down, calm down. I'd never do that. I want to help the people we live with, but I don't want to act like them.

DOG: You're right, Parrot. We'd never stoop that low.

CAT: Let's not lose our focus here. Paul and Jan take very good care of us. The least we can do is help them out.

PARROT: But if I start telling them what to do, I'll be just like them.

DOG: No, no, just tell them how we get along with each other. Then maybe they'll figure it out for themselves.

CAT: That's asking an awful lot from humans.

DOG: No, I think they could do it. They have pretty good brains. They've figured out a lot more stuff than we have.

PARROT: Except how to get along with each other. They're years behind us there.

CAT: Okay, okay (yawn) . . . I'm getting very sleepy here. So, bird, are you really going to talk to them?

PARROT: I'll do it tonight after the kids go to bed, and I'm counting on both of you to help me.

CAT: All right, but don't forget to let out a few squawks before you start. I wouldn't want to snooze through this for anything.

Scene Two

It is now about nine that same evening. Cat and Dog are on a small couch napping. Parrot is on his perch just behind the couch. Jan is sitting in her big chair reading a magazine. Paul is in his big chair dozing. The television is on as background noise.

PARROT: (*Squawking first and then saying in a loud voice*) Would you please turn off that television? We have some very important things to say to you.

JAN:	(*Very excited*) Paul, wake up, turn off the TV. Turn it off. Am I hearing things or did that parrot just say, we have some very important things to say to you?
PAUL:	(*Yawning*) The only thing that senile bird ever says is, "Canaries are cute, but they can't talk." You've never been able to teach him anything else.
PARROT:	She's not hearing things. We have a lot to say to both of you.
PAUL:	(*Gasps*) He really is talking to us. I can't believe it.
PARROT:	You heard me all right. Cat, Dog, and I have been talking things over. We're worried sick because we've heard you two talking about a divorce. What we want to know is what happens to us if you guys split up?
CAT:	It's not just us. We're worried about your children. Kids can suffer a lot when parents get divorced.
DOG:	Yeah, divorce hurts everyone. It's one of the saddest things your species does.
PAUL:	How do you know what's going on between us?
JAN:	You're worried about our children. Well, we are too. If it weren't for them, we'd already be divorced.

PARROT: We've been watching your marriage go downhill for a while now. All we ever hear is criticizing, blaming, and complaining. No marriage can survive that. But we think we can help you if you'll listen.

JAN: You really want to help us? I can't believe my ears.

PARROT: What can't you believe?

PAUL: You're just animals. What can you possibly know about divorce?

PARROT: We really don't know anything about marriage or divorce. We stay together as long as we're happy. I once shared a large cage with five pairs of lovebirds. They only had eyes for each other. They were happy together for years.

DOG: Humans marry and get along for a while, but sooner or later they start to pick on each other. You explain it, Parrot.

PARROT: What we've noticed is that most of the time Paul starts it, and then Jan fights back.

CAT: Except for the times she gives him the silent treatment. That's the part I don't mind. I hate my nap disturbed.

JAN: I'm listening to a parrot, a cat, and a dog, I can't believe it. It's exactly what we do.

PAUL: Hey! I know what's going on here. I've seen

you talking to that senile parrot behind my back. He couldn't figure this out on his own. You put him up to blaming me for all our trouble.

JAN: (*With some fervor*) You actually think I put him up to this?

PAUL: I wouldn't put it past you.

JAN: I'm plotting with a parrot against you. I've always thought you were crazy, but now I have witnesses.

PARROT: Paul, Paul, we're not plotting against anyone. We just don't want you and Jan to get a divorce.

CAT: It's so simple. Just treat each other the way you treat us.

DOG: Woof, Woof.

PARROT: He has trouble talking when he gets upset.

DOG: You treat us better than you treat your own children. I just don't understand that.

JAN: Paul, they're right. I've often said to myself— if only you'd treat me and the kids like you treat those animals. All you do is criticize us. You never criticize them.

PAUL: I only criticize you because I'm trying to help you. I complain because you don't listen to me. It's your fault our marriage is in shambles.

JAN: *(Appealing to the animals)* You see what I'm up against?

CAT: Meow, Meow, Meow.

JAN: What did she say?

PARROT: She's surprised you've put up with Paul as long as you have.

PAUL: All right, this has gone far enough. I'm warning you, Jan. You're going to have to choose between me and those animals. And you animals better be on my side or you're toast.

PARROT: Calm down, Paul. You're getting it all wrong. We aren't on Jan's side or your side. All three of us are on the side of your marriage.

DOG, CAT: That's right. That's right.

PARROT: You've been putting each other down for so long you've forgotten you're married.

DOG: But we haven't, Paul. *(Cat meows and nods her head in agreement)*

PAUL: What do you mean I've forgotten I'm married?

JAN: I think they mean that our complaining and all the bickering, the put-downs, everything we do, is killing our marriage. Let's face it. It's not only you; it's both of us. I guess we only think of ourselves.

PARROT: You used to love each other. We remember those days, even if you don't.

PAUL: But all married couples fight.

(Cat meows and makes other noises)

PAUL: Now what's she trying to say?

PARROT: Cat says you're mostly right. Married couples
           do a lot of fighting. But some don't; they get
           along fine. We could teach you how they do
           it if you'd be willing to learn.

PAUL: I'm a college graduate. I run a successful
           business. What could any of you possibly
           teach me?

JAN: Paul, marriage is not a business. You can
           never get away from it. Let's listen to them.
           We're miserable. What do we have to lose?

PAUL: I'm just having trouble with the idea that
           these animals claim to know more than I
           do.

JAN: But you can't deny that they get along better
           with each other than we do.

PAUL: *(Thinking)* No, I can't deny that. Maybe you're
           right. I guess we have nothing to lose.

JAN: Are you serious—you'll listen?

PAUL: Serious may be a little strong, but I'm will-
           ing to listen. Go ahead, Parrot.

PARROT: *(Pausing and thinking)* Whenever you feel
           like you want to criticize, blame, and com-
           plain . . .

DOG: Or nag, threaten, punish, or bribe. . . . Well,

before you do any of those things to each other . . .

CAT: Even before you roll your eyes, or use a demeaning tone of voice, or make a hostile gesture with your hands. Do you know what I mean?

JAN: I certainly do.

PAUL: I'm beginning to catch on. What should we ask ourselves?

PARROT: Ask yourselves, "Is what I am about to do going to harm **our** marriage?"

(Cat and Dog meow and woof to add emphasis)

PARROT: They are reminding me to tell both of you to think **our marriage**, never to think **my marriage**.

PAUL: Let me see if I understand you correctly. You're asking both of us to put our marriage ahead of what we want for ourselves.

PARROT: *(In a very loud voice)* **Correct, completely correct, that's the whole ball game.**

(Dog and Cat make noises in agreement)

PARROT: You want a divorce because for the last five years you've put what each of you wants ahead of your marriage. But if you stop doing that, you may be able to save your marriage.

PAUL: We try to do that with our children.

JAN: We almost always do it with our best friends.

PARROT: Most couples do that but not with each other. That's why we're so worried you may slip back to the criticizing and complaining.

JAN: But why, why will we? What you've taught us is so simple, and it makes perfect sense.

PAUL: I have to admit it makes sense. But why is it so hard to do when you're married?

PARROT: There is an answer to that question, but we're not sure you'll accept it.

JAN: Why won't we accept it?

CAT: Because you're human. You're deeply involved in the idea of right and wrong. If you don't get your way, you think it's right to take over and try to control everybody, when the only person you can really control is yourself.

PARROT: It gets so bad people even get violent. You've had violent thoughts, Paul. We've seen how angry you get.

PAUL: But she drives me, oops . . . I've got to stop thinking that way, but it's so hard.

JAN: That's the difference between you animals and us people, isn't it? You don't think you know what's right for others; we do.

PAUL: Do you explain things like this to other people?

DOG: Believe me, we're not into marriage counsel-

	ing. We just want to live here happily in this nice house with you and your family.
PARROT:	We appreciate how well you treat us, but your species is driven by power and ours isn't.
DOG:	Yeah! You sure don't live and let live.
CAT:	But we do, and it's a great way to live your life.
JAN:	I've never heard anyone come right out and say it like that, but I guess we are control freaks, aren't we?
PARROT:	You haven't heard it because you've never talked to an animal.
PAUL:	But do we have to be this way?
PARROT:	No, you don't. You can choose to be just as kind and considerate as we are. You certainly treat us that way.
JAN:	You mean that we can actually choose to treat each other better.
PARROT:	Of course you can, if you want to. Now, tell me what you have both learned.
PAUL:	I've learned that the only person I can control is me. I can't control Jan or, for that matter, anyone else.
JAN:	We've both learned we can control only our own behavior.
PARROT:	What happens if you try to control another person?

JAN: Whether we succeed or not, we harm our relationship. We've been doing that successfully for the past five years.

CAT: If you can actually learn to practice this, you will have learned something that ninety percent of your species has yet to learn. But now I'm getting really sleepy. I strongly suggest we all go to bed.

PAUL: Sounds good to me, but before we do, I just want to say thanks, you guys.

JAN: Me too.

Whatever Sarah and Jim's problem is, the way they are behaving toward each other is leading them in the same direction as Paul and Jan, the couple in the skit. Both couples have been dancing around the issue of divorce. They're in the danger zone, heading for the point of no return. Their children are in the line of fire. They would all like to do something about it, but they don't know what to do. Not knowing what to do makes divorce seem their only option. The whole family learning how to behave differently toward one another is the only answer.

✳

The question for you to discuss for this lesson is **What can this little skit teach your family?**

"MY HUSBAND STARES DUMBFOUNDED AT EVERY PRETTY GIRL. IS IT OK TO CLOBBER HIM?"
No, its really not his fault. Fact: Men are "hardwired" to look at pretty girls. Instinct is to look for a partner that will provide the man the best offspring. Just because he has a partner he loves doesn't stop the genetic programming. As Carl Jung said, "One must be able to let things happen."

Gordon and Mercedes' Story

I've been worried about my relationship with Mercedes. Our sex life has been slowly and steadily going downhill. I guess I'm just not as attracted to her as I used to be. Maybe I don't love her anymore. It's getting more and more difficult to maintain an erection when we have sex. Maybe I should get some Viagra, or better still maybe I should get a girlfriend.

Sex with Mercedes has become incredibly boring, and she isn't as interested in it as she used to be either. We talk about it once in a while, and she says what's happening to us is what happens to most married couples, as if she's an authority now on marriage. She claims I shouldn't be concerned, but I am. The only reason why I'm not having an affair is I'm afraid I won't be able to get it up with somebody else and be embarrassed.

We never do anything new. She's so traditional. When I suggested trying something different, she acted like she was insulted. All I know is I want more, and I'm not getting it. She says we have a good marriage, a happy family, a lot of nice friends. We do have a very active social life, and she's such a good hostess that everyone enjoys coming to our place.

But when we all get together, we're like a bunch of old married couples. The men are in one room talking about sports or politics, and the women are in another room talking about whatever women talk about.

Sometimes I wish we could do like in that movie *The Ice Storm* and put all our keys in a bowl. We could go home with whoever belongs to the keys we pick. At least we'd be doing something exciting for a change. I have other sexual fantasies I won't tell anybody about, much less Mercedes. She'd have a fit if I told her what they are. She's really a great wife in many ways, but I want more than a homemaker. I want a hot sexual partner.

I feel sorry for Gordon. I think he has that thing they call erectile dysfunction on TV. Now he wants to do all these weird and kinky things with me when we have sex. I think he thinks it's my fault. I don't think it is because we used to have great sex when we first got married. I don't know what happened. Sometimes I just don't act interested in having sex because I don't want to embarrass him. I know he feels bad every time he loses his erection, but how's that my problem? I used to like sex. He was a really affectionate lover and very considerate of my feelings. He used to write me love notes and put them on my pillow. One time I found myself surrounded by rose petals when I woke up in the morning. I truly don't know what changed. I'd love to have the old Gordon back.

I'm beginning to resent this new version of Gordon. He seems so self-centered now. All he thinks about is trying to get me to do things to him that to me seem degrading. I don't want to do these things, and I told him so. He gets so frustrated with me that he just pushes me away and turns over and goes to sleep. Well, I'm frustrated too. I used to like what we did. It worked for me. What's happened to us?

Maybe this happens to every married couple after they've been married as long as we have. I told him it's probably the most normal thing in the world. But I know he's not happy, and now that I think about it, I guess I'm not that happy either. There is always this pressure on both of us to perform, and when we don't, we feel bad about ourselves and each other.

I wish things could change. I told him we should just go on with our lives and forget about it. It's not that important in the grand scheme of things, is it? When you think about it, sex only takes up a small portion of our lives together. We do lots of other things that are fun and exciting.

I just hope our relationship can survive this little glitch. I'm worried though that Gordon might go for some outside sexual release or get addicted to Internet porn. I've heard all about that problem on talk shows. That would disappoint me very much. I made a commitment to him when we got married. I've been completely faithful to him our entire marriage, even though I have every reason to be dissatisfied.

When push comes to shove, I think I'm right and he's wrong. He wouldn't agree with me. He thinks he knows more than I do about this, but to argue with him about it would make things only worse.

– LESSON EIGHT –
Try New Ways to Improve
Your Sexual Intimacy

Satisfying sex is a necessary ingredient in a long happy marriage. It is not how often you do it or how long it lasts that's important, but it is very important that every time you make love both partners have a satisfying experience. Gordon and Mercedes are complaining that their sex life is not satisfying for either of them. They have almost given up on sex with each other altogether.

It is quite possible that you still have a sexual relationship with each other, but in an unhappy marriage it is unlikely that this relationship is satisfying to both of you. It may not be satisfying to either of you. We do not claim to be experts on sex, but we have discovered a few things about marital sex that we want to share with both of you in this lesson.

First of all, married couples often have the mistaken perception that when their infatuation with each other wanes and their sexual desire for the other declines, they are no longer in love. Gordon is operating under this impression. He and Mercedes are unaware that when infatuation has run its course, creative sex and lasting love can begin to replace the waning infatuation.

While it is desirable that you both have an orgasm, it is not necessary that you climax together. This is how sex is usually described in "adult" novels between infatuated partners who have just met and don't know a thing about each other. There is a great deal of athleticism but not much love or tenderness in these encounters.

There are also a few other popular beliefs that have little relationship to the kind of sex that is within your grasp if you are getting along well with each other. Remember, a high percentage of the sexual experience takes place in your mind. You may not believe it, but men can have great orgasms even if they are not capable of an erection. The nerves that allow a man to have a satisfying orgasm are usually still intact in men who are not achieving an erection.

A patient loving wife can use her creativity to bring her husband to orgasm without an erection. But wives may not be willing to make this effort if their husbands haven't made the effort to bring them to a satisfying orgasm first. Therefore, sex between happily married people can alternate, first her and then him or vice versa. The husband will get aroused along with his wife even if he can't get an erection as he brings his wife slowly and gently to orgasm with any method she prefers and he is willing to perform.

Which method he uses is up to them both to decide. A willing, loving husband can become a sexual artist as he educates himself to bring his wife to climax. The key to sexual compatibility is mutual satisfaction; how you get there is not important. This information has eluded not only Gordon and Mercedes but most couples who are unhappily married.

There is no age limit to these activities, no necessity to use drugs to induce an erection. No need to hurry, worry about timing, or be fearful of inadequacy or rejection. Mercedes complained that she and Gordon feel under a lot of pressure to perform sexually, as if they are in a competition or contest.

Sexual performance becomes pressure when you feel disconnected in your relationship, but if you are happy together and feel connected, orgasm becomes a gift you share with each other without judgment of yourself or evaluation of the other. Sex without preconceived expectations becomes, more often than not, a relaxing and enjoyable experience. Pressure to perform is linked to external control used on yourself, which keeps your mind focused on the performance rather than the enjoyment. That is why Mercedes suggested having less sex or forgetting about it altogether.

Just the knowledge there will be an orgasm available for

each of you almost every time will keep sex on both your minds. Understanding each other's physiology and individual sexual cycles is part of the fun of getting to know each other better in this new and exciting stage of intimacy beyond infatuation.

Gordon is thinking about experimenting with someone else, but he hesitates because he fears Mercedes will find out. Also, he's smart enough to be aware of the dangers of an illicit affair. He needs to communicate with Mercedes in a way that she will not tune him out. She needs for him to woo her with loving care first until she is ready to entertain any suggestions from him.

This will not be easy and could take a lot of patience on his part because right now her mind is all but closed to anything new. At any rate, the loving conversations, the tenderness and affection, need to happen first before any sexual exploration occurs.

A loving marriage is completely private. Anything sexual goes, as long as the partners agree. There are products on the market that are somewhat educational in that they show both partners who agree to share them together, what's out there in the sexual universe that they may safely try. The key phrase in this lesson is **they should both agree.** If they do not agree initially, they should both be patient, openminded, and negotiate a solution. However, neither should use any external control to try to get a sexual advantage by manipulating or rejecting the other. When Mercedes refused to do what Gordon suggested they do in bed, he got angry and turned his back to her in an attempt to control her with his anger and rejection. It didn't work.

We purposely made this the last lesson because all the previous lessons were meant to prepare you both for this one about sex. Nature has made sexual pleasure available to all of us. Married people can happily take advantage of this gift any time they choose. The purpose of this book has been to teach you what you need to do to be happy as a couple, not just as individuals. Enjoyable marital sex is a big part of that happiness. Happy couples continue to be interested in each other sexually. Marital happiness is the most effective aphrodisiac.

If in your marriage you have discovered things about sex that worked for you, don't let anything we have written here take precedence over what you have learned. Getting along better will just enhance what you have been doing. This book is written for people who believe they can learn how to move their marriage from where it is now to a better place for them.

Finally, if you both can feel completely relaxed, totally safe with each other and harbor no anger or resentment at each other, your likelihood of having a satisfying sexual relationship is very high. Sexual satisfaction in marriage depends on trust between partners. It also depends on doing everything possible to have a loving relationship all the time, not just in the bedroom. That is why the lessons in this book, which teach you how to get along better, can ultimately lead to a more intimate and sexually complete relationship between you. Sex is one way you can feel really close, intimate, and connected. There is nothing in this book that will hurt either of you if you both agree to follow the lessons and love each other.

– A FINAL WORD –

A happy marriage is a totally sharing relationship. As much as it may seem wise at times to withhold information about a severe illness or a financial setback from the other, loving partners rarely do this. Whether the news is good or bad, the first person they turn to is their partner. What this does is establish a level of trust unique to the kind of marriage we wanted to help you create when we decided to write this book together.

In our marriage we both know that no matter what happens, the other will want to become involved. Neither of us will ever be left alone under any circumstances. To attempt to protect the other, as we might protect a child or an elderly parent from uncomfortable news, is not a part of our love. We want to be completely involved. We take comfort not only from our belief that we want to be trusted with every problem but also from our belief that we will be a willing part of any solution.

This did not happen instantly. It built slowly as the marriage continued. As it did, the strength of our relationship grew with it. In time, ours became a very strong marriage. Its strength is a foundation that our family, friends, and even colleagues have learned to depend on. We take a great deal of joy in what we have created.

We have no further words. We appreciate your willingness to read this book. We look forward to hearing from you. You can write us at our e-mail address: wginst@wglasser.com. We will try to answer all your inquiries, but please wait until you have read all eight lessons before you write.

COUNSELING WITH CHOICE THEORY:
The New Reality Therapy
ISBN 978-0-06-095366-9 (paperback)

In this continuation of *Reality Therapy*, Dr. Glasser takes readers into his consulting room and illustrates exactly how he puts his popular therapeutic theories into practice.

REALITY THERAPY IN ACTION
ISBN 978-0-06-019535-9 (hardcover)

"In this age of managed care . . . reality therapy might be a better alternative to expensive psychiatric drugs." —*Library Journal*

CONTROL THEORY IN THE PRACTICE OF REALITY THERAPY: Case Studies • Edited by Naomi Glasser
ISBN 978-0-06-096400-9 (paperback)

A collection of case studies and examples of how Control Theory can translate into the practice of Reality Therapy.

THE CONTROL THEORY MANAGER
ISBN 978-0-887-30719-5 (paperback)

Combining Control Theory with the wisdom of W. Edwards Deming, this indispensable management resource explains both what quality is and what lead managers need to do to achieve it.

THE QUALITY SCHOOL: Managing Students Without Coercion
ISBN 978-0-06-095286-0 (paperback)

An examination of coercive management as an educational problem.

THE QUALITY SCHOOL TEACHER:
A Companion Volume to *The Quality School*
ISBN 978-0-06-095285-3 (paperback)

How to establish warm, totally non-coercive relationships with students, teach only useful material, and promote student self-evaluation.

SCHOOLS WITHOUT FAILURE
ISBN 978-0-06-090421-0 (paperback)

Dr. Glasser offers daring recommendations to stimulate educators.

POSITIVE ADDICTION
ISBN 978-0-06-091249-9 (paperback)

How to gain strength and self-esteem through positive behavior.

GETTING TOGETHER AND STAYING TOGETHER:
Solving the Mystery of Marriage • With Carleen Glasser
ISBN 978-0-06-095633-2 (paperback)

"A practical, insightful guide to loving, nurturing, and lasting relationships."

—John Gray, author of *Men Are from Mars, Women Are from Venus*